The Civilian

The Civilian

Oscar Porter

Copyright © 2018 by Oscar Porter.

Library of Congress Control Number:		2018907131
ISBN:	Hardcover	978-1-9845-3575-7
	Softcover	978-1-9845-3576-4
	eBook	978-1-9845-3577-1

All rights reserved. No part of this book may be reproduced or transmitted in any form or by any means, electronic or mechanical, including photocopying, recording, or by any information storage and retrieval system, without permission in writing from the copyright owner.

Any people depicted in stock imagery provided by Getty Images are models, and such images are being used for illustrative purposes only. Certain stock imagery © Getty Images.

Print information available on the last page.

Rev. date: 06/15/2018

To order additional copies of this book, contact:
Xlibris
1-888-795-4274
www.Xlibris.com
Orders@Xlibris.com
777450

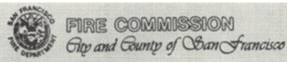

JAMES D. JEFFERSON, President
FRANK A. QUINN, Vice-President
HENRY E. BERMAN, Commissioner
SHARON L. BRETZ, Commissioner
TED N. SOULIS, Commissioner

260 GOLDEN GATE AVENUE
SAN FRANCISCO, CALIFORNIA, 94102
FAX NO. 929-1058
TELEPHONE (415)861-8000 EXT. 307
RAYMOND G. CONNORS, JR. Secretary

March 15, 1990

Mr. Oscar Porter
207 Skyline Boulevard
San Francisco, CA 94132

Re: Certificate of Merit

Dear Mr. Porter:

    Enclosed is the Certificate of Merit for the assistance you provided to the San Francisco Fire Department on May 26, 1989. The Fire Commission and Chief of Department appreciate your public-spirited involvement.

                                  Very truly yours,

                                  FIRE COMMISSION

                                  Raymond G. Connors
                                  Secretary

RGC:lq
Encl.

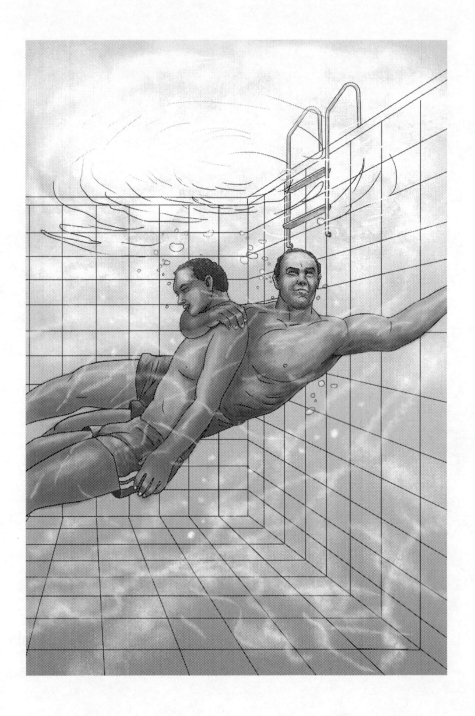

Courage from Within

When I was seven or eight years old, we were living in San Francisco, California, in a good home on Cook Street. We (my sisters and brothers and I) would be up late at night when my mother and father would be asleep.

One day, my sister Jo was trying to light the living room heater, when she set herself on fire while I was standing nearby. I ran to my mother and yelled that Jo was on fire; my mother put her on the floor and rolled her around until she was not burning anymore. I feel that when that happened, I started caring for others, and I did from that time on.

All my life, I have been involved in caring for people or saving lives. This is my story. Years later, I was at a pool party with my sisters and brothers, when we jumped into the pool one by one. While I was in the pool and underwater, I saw this guy passing by, trying to grab me. I didn't know that he couldn't swim. He was drowning! I came up for air, and everyone was yelling, "HE CAN'T SWIM! HE IS DROWNING!"

I looked into my sister's eyes and knew I had to do something. So I went back down into the water and found the guy still trying to reach the top of the pool from the bottom. I was in front of him. He was reaching out for me, and his eyes were open so wide I could see the fear. I knew that if he was to grab me, we would drown together, so I pushed him away from me, and I went behind him and put my two hands under his arms and pushed him upward and toward the top of the pool, and then I pushed him to the side and out of the pool. I then rolled him over and pushed water out of his body by pushing on the upper back toward the head. He had lots of water coming out of his mouth. He thanked me and said, "I will never forget what happened."

Two years later, I got a job as a counselor for at-risk teens at a ranch. During showers one day, I was in the towel room when a teen came in with a broken bottle in his hand and was walking toward another teen to cut or kill him. I was in the room at the time and saw him. I moved my body between him and the other teen and began to talk down the teen with the broken bottle. I was unable to call out for help because the towel room was near the shower area with the noise. No one could hear me. So I was there, standing face-to-face with a teen who wanted to hurt or kill another teen. I knew that I would have to fight this teen or talk him into dropping the broken bottle. I kept talking and looking in his eyes and not moving to the right or left. I did this for what seemed like fifteen minutes. He then threw the broken bottle out of the door. I walked him out of the towel room and up to the camp office. I then drove him to San Francisco and tested him for drugs. He had LSD in his system during the incident in the towel room at the ranch. I was lucky!

2009: The Car Pileup

I was coming home on Highway 280, driving on the left side of the highway, when I saw a car pulling over and stopping on the side of the highway, going the opposite way. I pulled over near the car and got out and began talking to the people in the car, telling them to get out and move about one hundred feet away from their car. As soon as they moved away from their car, another car came around the blind curve and hit their car! I ran over and helped the people out of the car. I told them to move away from the area. As soon as they moved away, another car came around the blind curve and also hit their car, causing the car to spin around. Again I ran over and helped the people out of the car, but the car door was unable to be opened on the driver's side.

I reached into the car and pulled both persons out. When this happened, another car came around the curb and hit the last car on the driver's side, spinning it out and to the other side of the highway.

It was raining hard that night with high winds. It was about 9:00 p.m. or later, and there were no lights. It was very dark on that highway. After seven cars piled up on the road, it stopped. No one was seriously hurt, and no one died that night! The fire department then came, and I then left and drove home safe. The next morning, I had a very bad headache because of the cars colliding near me!

Mother's Day

We just got back from Kaiser. That day, my mom was feeling fine—she was eating good and talking about how she spent the day at Kaiser. We parked in front of the house, and my mom was telling me how she was feeling dizzy. I got my mom out of the car and walked with her to the front of the house where the stairs were. Mom was talking, saying, "I am dizzy. I don't think I can make it up the stairs," so I sat Mom on the bottom of the stairs and went to get Daniel, my son, for help. When I returned, I saw my mom with her head down and not moving. I yelled to her, but she would not respond. I then started CPR and mouth-to-mouth, but Mom was sitting down, and my son Rafael's wife yelled down at me from the top of the stairs to lay her down flat. When I did that and applied CPR and mouth-to-mouth, Mom started to come back to life. I never thought I would be saving my own mother's life, but it happened. And she had another year to be with her family.

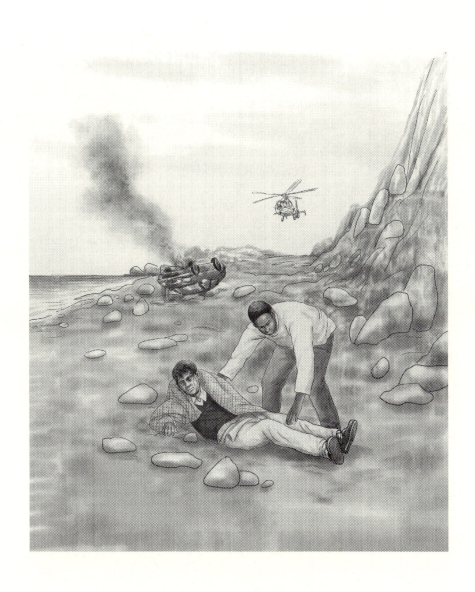

The Man over Devil's Slide

My son was about seven years old. We were coming from horseback riding, driving on Highway 1 in an area called Devil's Slide, when I saw a group of people standing on the side of the cliff, looking down at something. I stopped my car and walked over and saw a car that just went over and down, maybe eight hundred feet or more, to the beach. I asked the people around me what happened, and they stated that the car just went over. I left the babysitter with my son in the car and began to climb down the side of the cliff. The rocks and the dirt were very loose, so I had to be very careful not to fall off the cliffside. When I got down to the car, I saw one person out of the car and on the sand. I ran over and began talking to him. I did this in order to keep him aware of what happened. I could see large holes on his head area. He was thrown out of the car. I looked over at the car, and I could see gas and smoke coming from the tank. We had to move away from that area! I asked him if his legs were hurting. I then told him I had to move him away from the wrecked car; because of the gas leak, there could be a fire, so I used his pants and dragged him in the sand, away from the car and behind a large rock. I then ran back to the car and picked up the hood, which fell off when the car hit the sand, and used it cover us. I kept talking to him in order to keep him from going into shock or dying. It went on for what seemed like an hour or more. I then heard loud humming sounds. I looked up and saw the coast guard helicopter landing on the beach. They ran over and began caring for this person; they told me if I wasn't there to talk to him and care for him, he might not have lived.

The Head-On

One night while on my way to work for the 11–7 shift—I was driving on Highway 1 on the coast—I saw ahead of me red and blue lights going off and on. When I reached the area from where the lights were coming, I saw the sheriff and a truck that was on fire. I pulled over to the side of the road and didn't see anyone in the car or in the truck because their bodies were thrown out and onto the highway. The sheriff and I had to pick up the remains that were found on the ground and bag each body part. The man from the sheriff's department who was there asked me if I could help in picking up the human remains on the road and put them in small bags. This was something I was not prepared to do. What a night!

The Man at the Lake

One night when I was driving my van back to my job site in San Francisco, I came to a lake. It might have been 11:00 p.m. or twelve midnight when I saw a man standing in the middle of the road and holding his arm in the air, asking for help. The other hand was holding his neck. His white shirt had turned red because of the blood coming from his neck. Someone had cut his neck from ear to ear, causing a lot of blood to be lost. I stopped the van and told him to get inside; I was looking around to see if I could spot anyone in the area. I saw a black car parked about four hundred yards away with the lights turned off. He got into my van, bleeding from the neck down. I told him to keep his hand on his neck to slow down the bleeding and to sit behind me. I then told him to hold my hand and to squeeze it to let me know he was still okay. I drove off as fast as I could; I reached a red light but didn't stop because a life was on the line. As I was driving past the red light, I began thinking about the firehouse in the area. I turned around and drove to the house, yelling at him, "DON'T YOU DIE ON ME!"

When I got to the firehouse, I jumped out of the van and ran over to the large door of the firehouse and banged very hard a number of times. The door opened, and I yelled, "There is a man dying! MOVE IT! MOVE IT!"

The firemen came running from everywhere. We laid him on the ground, and they began to save his life. I held his head during this time, and for the very first time during this whole incident, I saw what had happened to his neck area. I could see a large cut, so wide that I could put my hand into it. It was as if you were cutting into a large steak. I could see all the layers of skin inside his neck, and blood was everywhere, but the firemen did not stop, and we saved his life that night. I went home and washed the blood off me, but I could not wash what happened off my mind. It would stain my memory forever.

Later I got a letter from the City of San Francisco. It was the chief of the firehouse and other members of the city rewarding me for my efforts that helped saved a life.

I saw the person I saved with the help of God and the fire department a few months later at the courthouse hallway. He didn't know who I was at the time, but when I told him my name, he broke down crying and told me he was so thankful for what I did that night. He stated, "Ask anything of me and I will give it!"

Most persons that I have had the honor to save from harm or death do not know me or will never see me again, but I am thankful to God for the honor of being there for them.

The Apartment Burning

I was driving in the Mission District at about 9:00 to 10:00 p.m. on a weekday, enjoying the drive, when I saw the red color of fire coming from an apartment. I drove toward the fire area, and when I got there, I could see people standing outside, looking at the fire. I pulled over and parked down the street from the fire. I could hear the sound of glass blowing up and people yelling in fear. I ran over to the apartment door. At the door were people running out, yelling and crying.

One policeman and I were standing at the door. I told the policeman that I must go in and help the people out. At that point, I ran into the burning apartment, looking for anyone who might need my help. As I was going up the stairs, I told people to get out. I ran from door to door, kicking down most and going into the apartment, looking for persons in need. I went from floor to floor. I had to climb the outside of the apartment, holding on to the pipe and whatever I had to use to get to the next floor. I could still hear people yelling and windows being blown out by the pressure of the fire. I reached the third floor and had to kick the back door in. I again went to every door inside each room, trying to hear calls. I then ran into firemen in the stairway, and they told me to leave the building. I was done, so I left.

Taken

I was going to SF State, driving on the other side of the highway wall, when I saw another car jump the small barrier between the highway and hit a small car head-on, causing the driver in the small car to be in pain and unable to move. She was hurt, and her head was bleeding. I ran over and wanted to help her out of the car, but she was pinned under the dashboard. All I could do was calm her down and keep her alive as long as I could. Then the firemen came. They had to cut the door in order to get her out. I had to leave, but when I drove by the area the next day, I saw a large area full of flowers. I started to cry and ask God why she was taken when he

(God) put me there to help that day. No one had ever died when I was involved in saving his or her life, so why now? Or maybe she didn't die after all. I will never know, and I guess that's okay.

Devil's Slide II

During the night on the way home from work, I was driving when I came to a few cars that had stopped. I got over and saw two cars that were involved in a head-on collision. One car was a convertible, and the driver was not in the car. He was thrown out of the car and into the woods. A few others and I began looking for the driver. I was pushing aside every brush with the fear of finding a body. We looked for about an hour. The helicopter then came with the bright lights but couldn't find the driver at the time either. This was not good. I could not find the driver. They called off the search that night, and I had to leave with a feeling of failure and disappointment.

The Truck Overturned

On the way to work at the airport, I was driving in my car when I saw a large cement truck making a sharp turn and rolling over on its side. I ran over and began to turn off the truck and wanted to help the driver, but he jumped out and ran away from the truck. The police came down. I then ran after the truck driver across the highway with cars moving at a high speed, running into landfills. I could not find the driver of the truck, so I returned to the overturned truck, and everyone was there—policemen, firemen, and EMTs. So I walked to my car and drove off!

Highway Child

I was coming from work one night, driving on I-280. It was very dark, when I came upon a car that stopped in the fast lane, but the car had its lights on, so I was thinking the car was moving. When I came upon the stopped car, I had to switch lanes very fast to not hit the car. I was going about sixty miles per hour. I then ran over to the car, and I saw one lady in the driver's seat. I asked if she was okay, and she said she was okay. I then told her to leave the car and let me help her to the side of the road. After she got to the side of the road, I asked her if there were more people in the car. She said, "My little girl is in the back, in a car seat." At this time, the highway was full of passing cars going about eighty to ninety miles per hour. I ran across the highway and removed the baby from the car seat and returned the baby to her mother. Sometime later, the highway patrol officers came and took care of the mother and her baby. Again it was a good night.

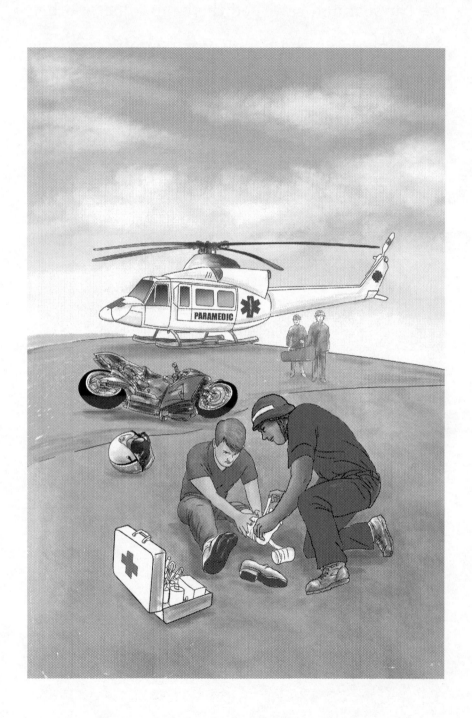

Motorcycle and Car, Highway 85

That day, the highway was empty. There were no cars. It was a wonderful day. I was driving on Highway 85 when I came up to a blind curve. During my turn, I came upon a motorcycle rider lying on the ground, yelling in pain. A car about fifty feet away was pulled over on the side of the road with its front window broken by the motorcycle helmet of the rider. The rider crossed over the lane and hit the front window and then was forced to the ground. He then slid about fifty feet away from the car. I pulled over and ran over to help. The motorcycle rider had his helmet on his head. The helmet was black, but there was a large, softball-size white shape on his helmet from hitting the ground with so much force and then sliding fifty feet that it took the color off the helmet. I could not remove his helmet because he could bleed to death or die from an exposed head injury. So I looked at his body to see if I could find any other injuries, and I did. His leg was so bad that his shinbone was pushing up and out his knee. He was yelling in pain. All I could do was keep him calm and slow the bleeding in his leg. Someone called 911, and the helicopter came.

Lane to Lane

I was driving my car late one night in the sunset area of San Francisco when I saw a car in front of me driving from lane to lane as if the car was out of control. I followed the car for about four blocks before I could think of a way to stop and remove the driver from the car without any harm. He had been drinking, so I followed the car to a red light. While the car was stopped, I jumped out of my car with an old map in my hand. I then ran to the car ahead of me and asked the driver to roll his window down because I was lost. I had the street map in my hand. Just as he rolled down the window, I reached in the car and pulled out the keys from the ignition and told the driver to get out of the car and put his hands on the car. I then began to pat down the driver. I told the driver to sit on the side of the road. He asked me if I was a police officer. I told him not to worry about that now and to stay calm. I was hoping the police would be driving around the area, but for ten minutes or more, they were not. But then I saw the police. I then explained what happened, and they took over.

Child Choking

We were eating at a birthday party, and the kids were running around the house. I was sitting near the doors, when a little child (boy) came near the door. He was choking on food and could not get the food out. No one seemed to notice him choking, so I picked him up and hit his upper back with my hand until the food was dislodged from his mouth. He then ran away happy, not knowing he would have had a bad day if he didn't pass that door where I was sitting.

Child Locked in Car

I was near the parking lot at San Francisco State University, when I heard a woman yelling very loudly and hysterically. I turned to look and saw her running toward me. I asked her what's wrong. She said, "My baby is in the car, and the car door is locked with the keys in the ignition." During the whole incident, I could hear the baby crying very loudly, and at the same time, the engine was racing very high and all the windows were up. The woman was just getting more hysterical. Just that month, I bought a slim jim, and I had a chance to use it. So I ran to my car and picked up the slim jim and raced back to the woman's car and worked on the door. With a little effort, the door opened. I turned off the engine and gave the woman her keys.

Trapped in an Upside-Down Car

While I was driving on a nice, clear day with my music up loud, I looked over at the ocean. I was looking at the dark-blue sky and the white-colored waves when something caught my eye. I looked to the left, and I saw a car turned upside down on the other side of the road. There was a young woman trapped inside the car, and she was hanging upside down, yelling and crying out loud. I went over to the left side of the car and had to climb inside the car and began to talk to her and calm the situation down. She was harming herself by yelling and crying uncontrollably. The mother was in the car, but when it turned upside down, she got out and sat on the curb nearby. I was keeping an eye on them because people can go in shock in situations like this.

Tree Fallen

One Saturday night, the sky was dark and the fog was everywhere, making it too hard to see more than five hundred feet ahead. I was driving on Highway 1 when I came to a turn on the road; there in front of my car was a very large tree that had fallen on the highway. I almost hit the fallen tree, which would have caused the cars behind me to hit me or go off the road after passing the tree. I got out of my car and got a flare. I then started to turn cars away from the fallen tree, which was blocking two lanes on the highway. Some cars were driving too fast and didn't see me standing next to the tree. They would come up to one hundred feet away before turning away from the fallen tree, which was lying across the highway. Eventually the police came and took over. It was a good night.

The Fall

I was in the gym and was enjoying being in the heated pool. I was in the pool for ten minutes when I saw a lady walking out the steam room toward the heated pool. I then saw her face become pale and her eyes roll back in her head and then close as she was falling backward, hitting the floor hard. Her head hit very hard, causing the lady to go unconscious for thirty-five seconds. She had stayed in the steam room too long, causing her to lapse into unconsciousness and to fall to the floor.

Another person and I remained with her until she became conscious.

She began talking to us, which was good. People called "all" for help from the fire and the paramedic unit.

They took her to the hospital that night. I hoped she was okay!

A Good Night!

Monday

January 22, 2018

I had a good Bible study the night of January 22, 2018. It was cold and dark on the highway, making it very hard to see ahead when driving a car or, worse, a motorcycle.

While I was driving home, I could sense something was wrong ahead, and then I saw lights flashing red. I saw a body lying on the ground about forty-five feet away from a motorcycle that hit a curb and flipped on its side.

I pulled over and turned off the lights of the car to avoid being hit by other cars on the highway.

I ran over to the person lying on the ground. I looked him over and asked, "Are you bleeding anywhere? Are you in any severe pain?"

THE JOURNEY CONTINUES . . .

Printed in the United States
By Bookmasters